What Can Live in the Ocean?

by Sheila Anderson

Lerner Publications · Minneapolis

An ocean is a **habitat**.

It is where plants and
animals live.

Ocean animals have special **adaptations**.

These help them live in the ocean.

Fish use fins to swim.

Gills let them breathe underwater.

Lobsters have claws.

They use them to grab fish.

Octopuses can change color.

This helps them hide.

Whales have **blowholes** on top of their heads.

Whales breathe through blowholes.

Some sea horses look like **seaweed**.

This helps them hide.

Sharks have lots of sharp teeth for eating fish.

What other adaptations help animals live in the ocean?

Penguin Adaptations

beak

flippers

layer
of
fat

short,
waterproof
feathers

Learn More about Adaptations

Penguins have short, waterproof feathers on their bodies. These feathers keep them dry. Penguins have flippers that work like fins for swimming. A layer of fat under their skin helps penguins stay warm. Their sharp beaks are perfect for catching fish. Yum!

Fun Facts

 Adult flounders have both eyes on one side of their heads. This makes it easy for them to see when they are lying flat on the ocean floor.

 Fish often swim in groups called schools. A hunting fish cannot see just one fish swimming in a group.

 Crabs have claws on the ends of their hands for catching fish.

 Sea turtles can hold their breath for hours.

 Fish have eyes on the sides of their heads so they can see all around them. This makes it easy to see hunters nearby.

 Eels have long, thin bodies that can fit in small areas between rocks.

 Some octopuses squirt ink when they are in danger. Hunters cannot see them through the inky cloud.

 There are fish that look like rocks, plants, or even sand!

Glossary

 adaptations – things that help a plant or animal live in a specific habitat

 blowholes – holes on top of the heads of whales and dolphins that they use to breathe air

 gills – an organ used to breathe underwater

 habitat – a place to live

 seaweed – a plant that grows underwater

Index

The images in this book are used with the permission of: © iStockphoto.com/Aldo Ottaviani, pp. 2, 22 (second from bottom); © iStockphoto.com/Stephan Kerkhofs, p. 3; © Prisma/SuperStock, pp. 4, 22 (top); © Reinhard Dirscherl/Visuals Unlimited, Inc., p. 5; © age fotostock/SuperStock, pp. 6, 8; © Stuart Westmorland/Riser/Getty Images, pp. 7, 22 (middle); © LESZCZYNSKI, ZIGMUND/Animals Animals, p. 9; © Ken Lucas/Visuals Unlimited, Inc., p. 10; © Serban Enache/Dreamstime.com, p. 11; © Paul A. Souders/CORBIS, pp. 12, 22 (second from top); © David Fleetham/Visuals Unlimited, Inc., pp. 13, 22 (bottom); © iStockphoto.com/Sara Kwong, p. 14; © David B Fleetham/Photolibrary/Getty Images, p. 15; © Pacific Stock/SuperStock, p. 16; © iStockphoto.com/Glenn Rose, p. 17; © Laura Westlund/Independent Picture Service, p. 18.

Front Cover: © Georgette Douwma/Photographer's Choice/Getty Images.

Lerner Publications Company
A division of Lerner Publishing Group, Inc.
241 First Avenue North
Minneapolis, MN 55401 USA

For reading levels and more information, look up this title at www.lernerbooks.com.

Library of Congress Cataloging-in-Publication Data

Anderson, Sheila.
    What can live in the ocean? / by Sheila Anderson.
       p.   cm. — (First step nonfiction—animal adaptations)
    Includes index.
    ISBN 978–0–7613–4569–5 (lib. bdg. : alk. paper)
    ISBN 978–0–7613–6253–1 (EB pdf)
    1. Marine animals—Adaptation—Juvenile literature. I. Title.
    QL122.2.A496 2011
    591.77—dc22   2009024859

Manufactured in the United States of America
3 - 38622 - 10526 - 5/10/2019